Boys' Day

Written and photographed by
Minako Ishii

www.beyondbordersimages.com

3565 Harding Avenue
Honolulu, Hawai'i 96816
toll free: (800) 910-2377
phone: (808) 734-7159
fax: (808) 732-3627
e-mail: sales@besspress.com
www.besspress.com

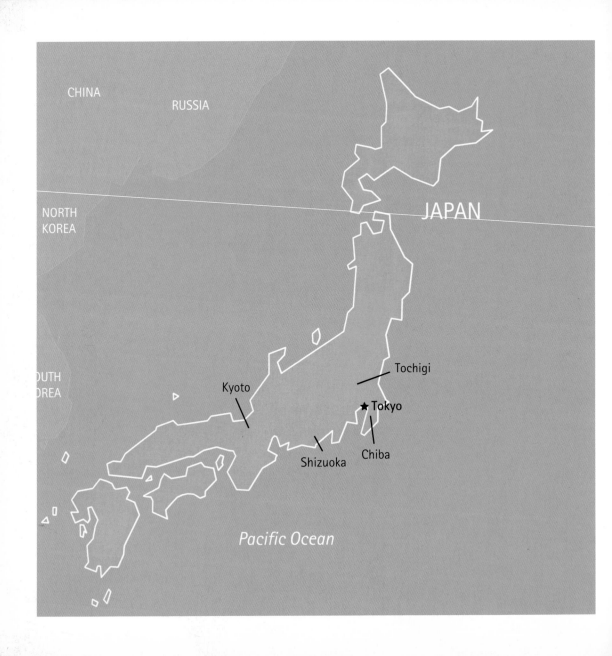

For the children of Hawai'i and Japan who carry on the old traditions.
May your carps become dragons.

Tango no Sekku, the Boys' Festival, began in China, but it has been a Japanese custom for over a thousand years. Since 1948, May 5 has been celebrated in Japan as both Boys' Day and Children's Day.

Long ago, to honor their sons, Japanese samurai (warriors) flew banners bearing their family crest above the gateway to their homes. Other families hung *koi-nobori* (carp streamers) above their gates, hoping that one day their sons would become samurai. The carp became a symbol of Boys' Day. Above is a *musha* (warrior) doll.

From the end of April through May 5, *koi-nobori* fill the skies of Japan. Carp are strong fish that fight their way upstream. Flying the carp streamers encourages boys to work hard to reach high goals.

A Chinese legend says only the carp that successfully swim to the Dragon's Gate waterfall on the Yellow River can become dragons. One of the few people in Japan who make carp streamers by hand says of his carp, "I do not draw ordinary carp, but carp before they turn into dragons!"

In Tochigi, hundreds of carp fly over the river.

Kindergartners walk with their teachers beside the river. As they walk, they sing a song: "Carp streamers are high above roofs; the biggest carp is the father, and the smaller carp are children. They're enjoying swimming in the sky."

At the annual opening ceremony of Children's Week in Tokyo, the champion *sumotori* hands out carp to children and joins in flying larger carp.

On Boys' Day some families fly carp kites. In their homes, they display symbols of strength: a *kabuto* (samurai helmet), swords, bows and arrows, or a *musha* doll.

The iris *(shobu)*, with its sword-shaped leaves, is also a part of Boys' Day celebrations. Families hang *shobu* under their eaves or take baths sprinkled with *shobu* leaves.

Families in Hawai'i also celebrate Boys' Day, to wish their boys health and happiness. The custom was brought to Hawai'i by early Japanese plantation workers.

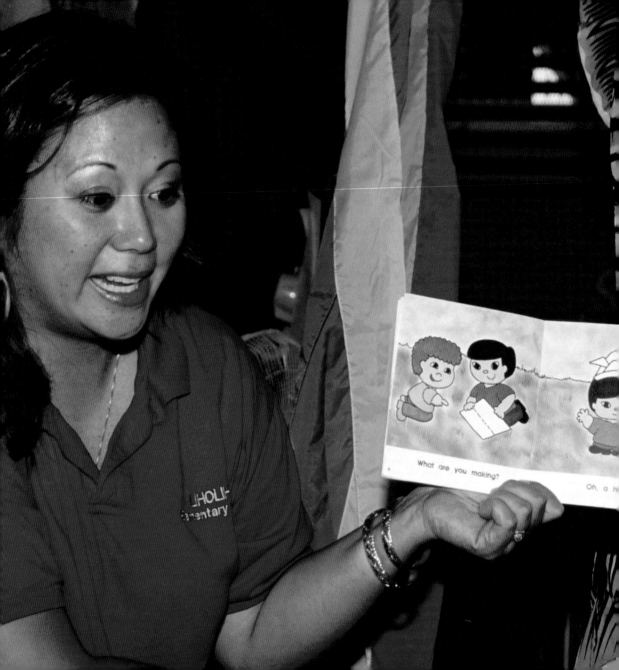

On Boys' Day, Hawai'i schoolchildren learn about Japanese culture and food. They make *kabuto* (above), and learn Japanese words. "What does *oishii* [yummy] mean?" the teacher asks. A child replies, "SPAM®!"

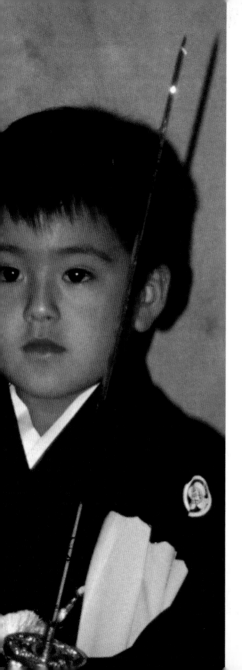

Boys in Hawai'i dress like samurai and pose for photos.

Foods eaten on Boys' Day have special meanings. *Kashiwa-mochi* (rice cakes) filled with sweet bean paste and wrapped in oak leaves are shaped like *kabuto*. The oak stands for strength. *Chimaki* (rice dumplings) are wrapped in bamboo leaves and tied with a Chinese reed. The bamboo stands for loyalty.

Whether it is called Boys' Day or Children's Day, May 5 is a day to honor children.

Glossary

carp streamers: On Boys' Day, some families fly one carp for every boy in the household. Others fly a carp for the father and for the girls in the household, too.

chimaki: rice dumplings.

kabuto: samurai helmet.

kashiwa-mochi: rice cakes.

koi-nobori: carp streamers.

musha: dolls made for display on Boys' Day. Many of them are dressed as warriors.

oishii: yummy.

samurai: professional warriors, who were members of Japan's aristocracy, or upper class.

shobu: iris.

sumotori: Japanese wrestler.

Tango no Sekku: the Boys' Festival, celebrated today as Boys' Day.

Tochigi: a prefecture (district) on the island of Honshu, Japan. The district is known for its ski resorts, temples, and hot springs.

Yellow River: a three-thousand-mile-long river in northeastern China.

yokozuna: the top rank in sumo (a Japanese form of wrestling in which one wrestler tries to make the other fall or step outside the ring).

Glossary

Chiba: a prefecture (district) and a city on the island of Honshu, Japan. Narita Airport and Tokyo Disney Resort are located in Chiba prefecture.

Hina Matsuri: the Doll Festival, also known as Girls' Day.

hishi-mochi: diamond-shaped rice cakes.

kimono: a floor-length Japanese robe with wide sleeves. It is worn with an obi, a wide sash tied in the back in a large, flat bow.

Kyoto: a prefecture (district) and a city on the island of Honshu, Japan. The city of Kyoto was once the capital of Japan and is known as a cultural and religious center.

Shinto: a religion that began in Japan. Followers worship nature spirits and ancestors.

Shizuoka: a prefecture (district) and a city on the island of Honshu, Japan. The district is known for its green tea, strawberries, and mandarin oranges, and as the location of Mt. Fuji.

sushi: cooked rice seasoned with vinegar. It is shaped into pieces or rolls, and is often combined with raw or cooked fish, egg, or vegetables, or wrapped in seaweed.

taiko: Japanese drum.

At the most beautiful time of year, Girls' Day announces the arrival of spring. Flowers bloom as Hawai'i and Japan celebrate their cultural values across the Pacific Ocean.

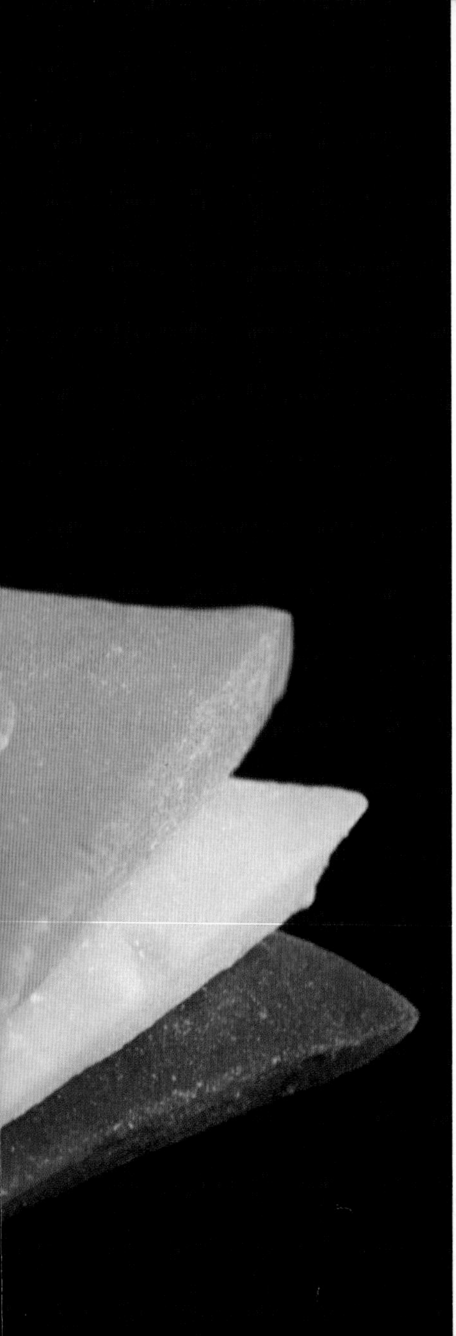

One thing that must be eaten on this day is *hishi-mochi*, colorful diamond-shaped rice cakes. The top layer of *hishi-mochi* stands for the peach blossom of spring. The middle layer stands for the white snow of winter. The bottom layer stands for the grass of early summer. Nisshodo Candy Store workers in Honolulu start making *hishi-mochi* at two in the morning to fill orders for Girls' Day.

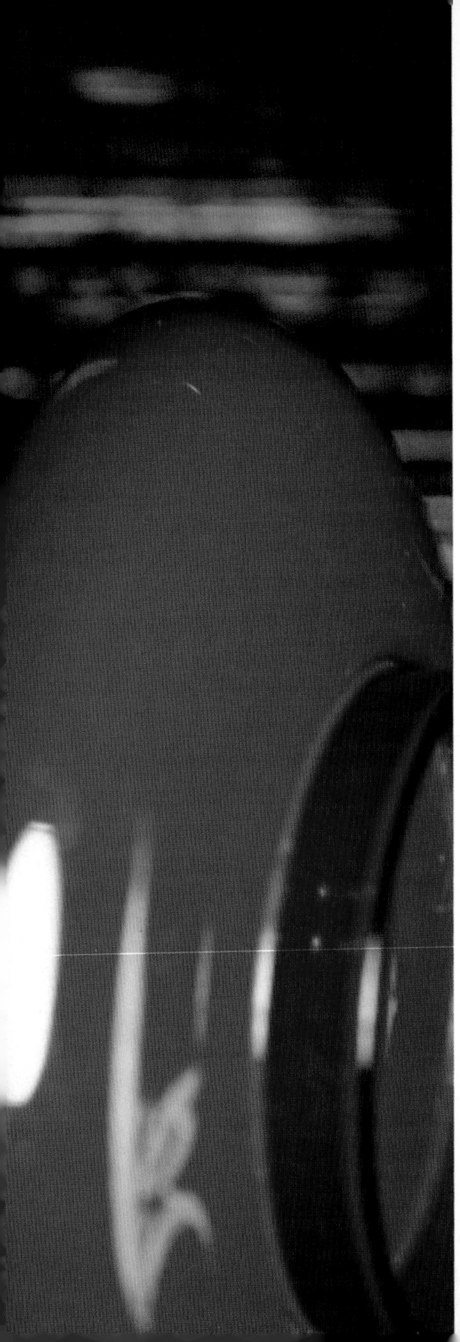

Sushi (above) and clam soup (left) are often served on Girls' Day.

At some schools, girls get to eat lunch before the boys do. At left, a teacher cooks her grandmother's soup recipe with help from her Japanese language students. Above, a student eats a special dish.

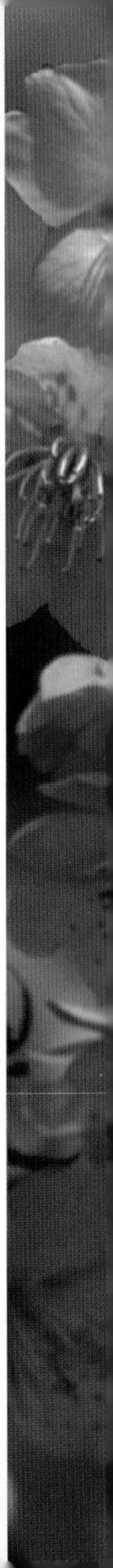

Boys celebrate Girls' Day, too.

Happy Girl's Day March 3rd

Girls learn about Girls' Day by drawing and coloring Japanese dolls.

Girls in Hawai'i celebrate, though not in the same way that Japanese girls do. It is a day for families to show their love for their daughters Hawaiian style.

Hawai'i also celebrates Girls' Day. March 3 is a day for families to honor their daughters and wish them health and happiness. At home and at school, children learn about Japanese customs.

Young girls dress up in beautiful kimonos, like the ones the dolls wear. According to tradition, they must put the dolls away after March 3 if they want to get married someday.

In one room of their house, Japanese families display a set of dolls and doll furniture from the ancient royal court. The dolls are handed down through the mother's family from generation to generation. The furniture is a symbol of a happy future marriage.

In Shizuoka, grandmothers make hanging dolls (above and at left, in front of a traditional kimono) for their granddaughters. The designs represent the grandmothers' wishes for their granddaughters. The crane and the turtle stand for long life. The *taiko* (drum) stands for good fortune. The plum stands for purity, and the bamboo stands for growth.

Girls' Day is an important holiday in Japan today. People celebrate it in many ways. In Chiba, more than twenty thousand dolls sit on the sixty steps of a shrine. Above, a young woman performs a Shinto dance.

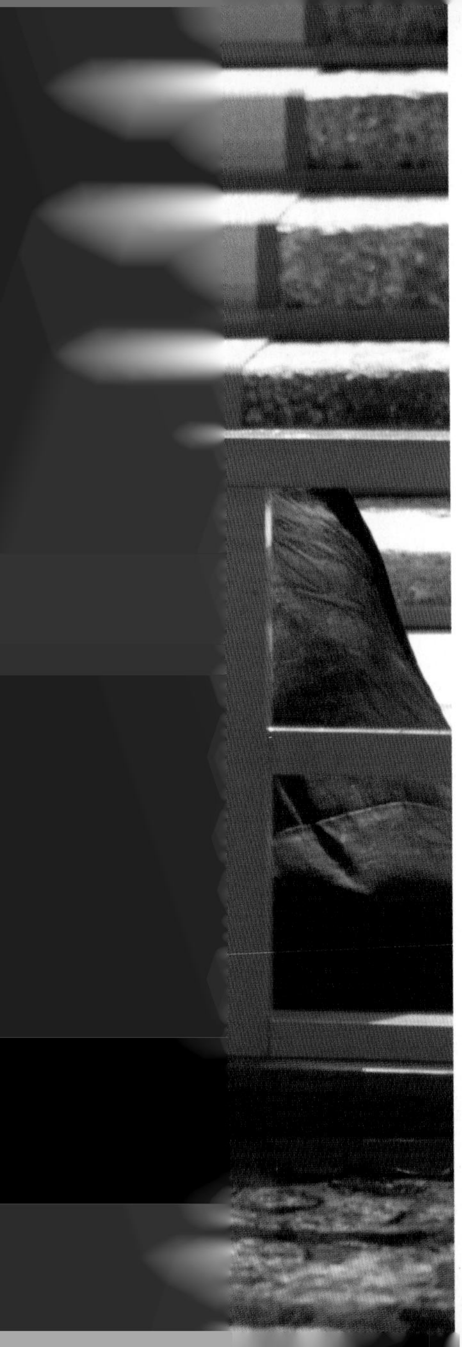

Around four hundred years ago, the common people in Japan began celebrating Girls' Day. Over time, the customs changed. They became mixed with Shinto religious customs. In Kyoto, dolls are set afloat on a river in straw "boats." People believe that the dolls carry people's troubles away with them.

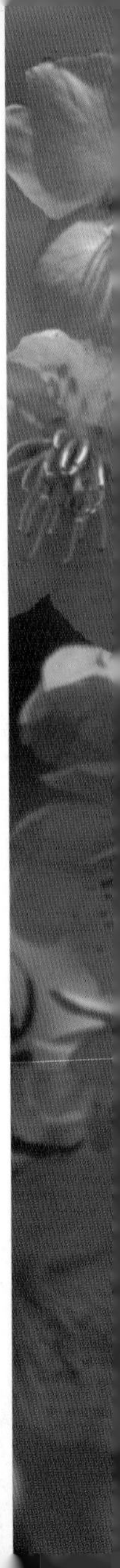

Girls' Day is celebrated on March 3. It is also known as Hina Matsuri (Doll Festival). It began in China as a religious ceremony. Japanese nobles adopted the custom over a thousand years ago.

For my lovely nieces, Naho, Hazuki, Ayano, and May; for my photography students at Waikīkī Elementary; and for the girls of Hawai'i and Japan. All springs bloom, and so will you.

Acknowledgments

Heartfelt gratitude to the following:

My parents Kinji and Kazumi and sister Mamiko, who encouraged me to follow my heart; and Rusty, who believed in me and supported me always.

Mrs. Takagi, Mika, Naho, Hazuki, Ayano, and May, for celebrating Girls' Day with me; Edgar, Kimberly, Austin Kekai, Keara Kamalani Ortega, and Keara's friends Mike and Tyra Harada, for adding beautiful smiles to the book; David, Alicia, and Troy Brandt, Kaipo, Kayte, Kanani, and Lani Guerrero, AJ, Patricia, Marissa, and Jordan Halagao, Amika and Kieko Matterson, and Robert Perkinson, Albert and Austen Andrade, and Robyn Kuranaga, Fusetaro, Miwa, Kotaro, Shintaro, and Nodoka Fuse, for letting me come into their lives.

Brandy Aylward, Joan Berkowsky, and their students; Charlotte Unni, Christine Kinau Gardner; Diana Arakawa and their students; and Kelley Espinda and her students, for providing the great activities.

Michael Hirao and Bobbie, for mochi from the Nisshodo Candy Store in Kalihi, O'ahu; and Shayna Coleon and the Japanese Cultural Center in Honolulu, for offering opportunities for the children of Hawai'i to enjoy Japanese traditions.

Shimogamo Shrine in Kyoto Prefecture, Tomisaki Shrine in Chiba Prefecture, and the Ministry of Health, Labor, and Welfare of Japan, for preserving traditional rituals. Takashi Hashimoto of Hashimoto Yakichi Shoten in Saitama Prefecture, for sharing stories of carps and Boys' Day.

Gregg Merci of Lightwaves for helping me with fast film development. Last but not least, Buddy Bess for giving me this wonderful opportunity to work on such a special project that is so dear to my heart. I am eternally grateful. Revé Shapard and Carol Colbath for being very helpful and patient with me.

Design: Carol Colbath

Library of Congress Cataloging-in-Publication Data

Ishii, Minako.
  Girls' Day/Boys' Day / Minako
Ishii.
        p.   cm.
    Includes illustrations, glossary.
    ISBN: 978-1-57306-274-9
    1. Festivals—Hawaii—Pictorial
works—Juvenile literature. 2. Festivals—
Japan—Pictorial works—Juvenile literature.
3. Hawaii—Social life and customs—Pictorial
works—Juvenile literature. 4. Japan—
Social life and customs—Pictorial works—
Juvenile literature. 5. Hina matsuri—
Juvenile literature. 6. Kodomo no hi—
Juvenile literature. 7. Children's Day
(Japan)—Juvenile literature. I. Title.
GT4896.H3.I58 2007   394.2-dc21

Printed in China

Girls' Day

Written and photographed by
Minako Ishii

www.beyondbordersimages.com

3565 Harding Avenue
Honolulu, Hawai'i 96816
toll free: (800) 910-2377
phone: (808) 734-7159
fax: (808) 732-3627
e-mail: sales@besspress.com
www.besspress.com

BESS PRESS